Why it works

Pushes and Pulls

Anna Claybourne

QEB Publishing

Author Anna Claybourne
Consultant Terry Jennings
Editor Louisa Somerville
Designer Susi Martin
Picture Researcher Claudia Tate
Illustrator John Haslam

Publisher Steve Evans
Creative Director Zeta Davies

Picture credits (fc = front cover, t = top, b = bottom, l = left, r = right)

pic credits to come

Library of Congress Control Number: 2008011713

ISBN 978 1 59566 558 4

Printed and bound in China

Words in **bold** can be found in the glossary on page 22.

Contents

On the move

Things are moving all the time. Birds and airplanes fly through the air. Leaves flutter in the wind. Cars zoom along roads. Rain falls from the sky.

But why? What makes things move?

Try this

You need a small ball. Place the ball on a table top. Now see how many ways you can make it move.

In a game of soccer, the ball moves around all the time.

Throw it. (Gently!)

Drop it.

4

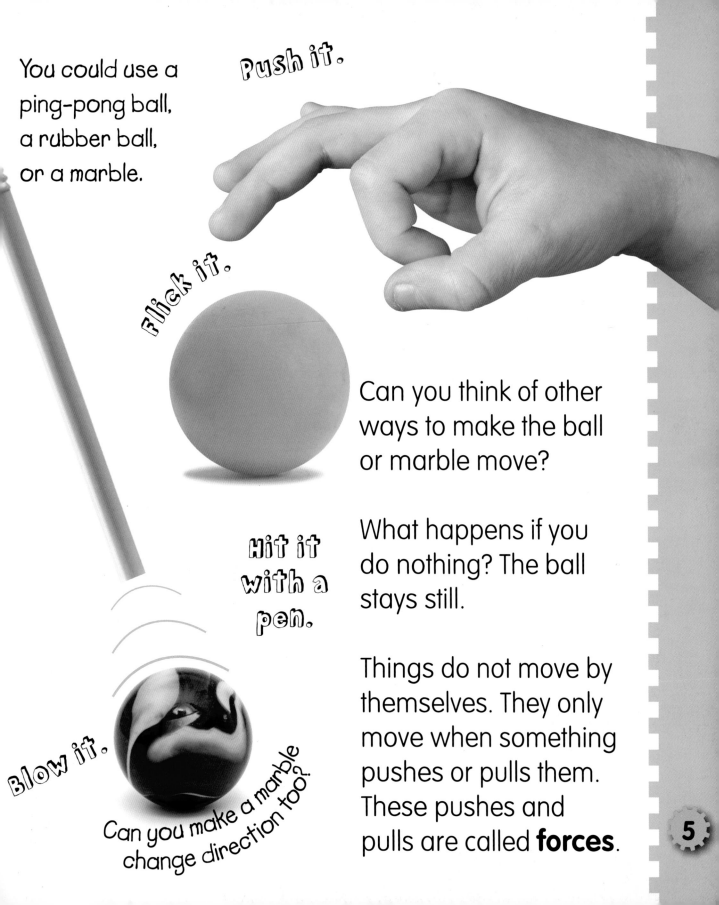

You could use a
ping-pong ball,
a rubber ball,
or a marble.

Push it.

Flick it.

Hit it
with a
pen.

Blow it.

Can you make a marble
change direction too?

Can you think of other
ways to make the ball
or marble move?

What happens if you
do nothing? The ball
stays still.

Things do not move by
themselves. They only
move when something
pushes or pulls them.
These pushes and
pulls are called **forces**.

Pushing and pulling

Pushes and pulls can make toy cars move. Here is an experiment that you can try with some friends.

Try this

You need a car for each person. Use cars that are all about the same size.

2 On the count of three, everyone has to push their car as hard as they can.

1 Line up your cars in a big space, such as in a school hall, on a kitchen floor, or in a corridor.

Whose car goes fastest and farthest?

3 What happens if you stick two cars together? Push the first car along. The second car gets pulled along with it.

Stick the front of one car to the back of another with tape.

It's a fact

A car can move if it is pushed or pulled. The harder you push or pull, the faster it goes.

STRETCH AND SQUEEZE

Pushes and pulls can make things move in other ways too. Squeezing a piece of modeling clay is a type of push. Stretching the clay is a kind of pull. Squeezing and stretching makes the clay change shape.

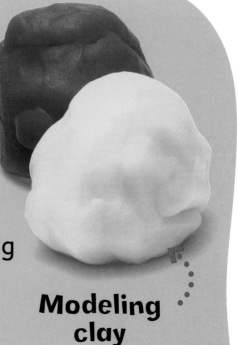

Modeling clay

Stopping

Pushes and pulls don't just make things move. They make them change direction or slow down and stop, too.

What would happen if you pushed a toy car along the floor and it hit another, upturned car?

BANG.

The upturned car makes your car stop by pushing against it. Even though the other car is not moving, it has a pushing force that stops your car.

ry this

Roll a ball (or a marble) along a table. Try to stop it with different things.

Which of these things stop the ball?

A book?

Your hand?

A dangling strip of paper?

Marble

When you block the ball's way, you make a pushing force. If the force is strong enough, it pushes against the ball and stops it.

It's a fact

The pushing force of the paper is not as strong as the pushing force of the moving ball. So the ball doesn't stop.

Dropping

If you hold up a ball and let go of it, what does it do? When you let go, the ball falls to the ground.

Most objects fall to the ground when you drop them. If you jump up, you fall back down, too.

Objects fall because something is pulling them. This pulling force is called **gravity**. It pulls things toward the center of the Earth—the **planet** we live on.

When you jump, gravity pulls you back to Earth.

There is very little gravity in space, so an astronaut floats about.

The Earth's gravity pulls things toward it. It pulls you down, so that you stand on the ground, instead of floating away.

I WONDER WHY?

We know how gravity works. But we don't know why it happens! Scientists are still trying to find out.

Getting faster

As an object drops or rolls downhill, it speeds up and goes faster and faster. This is because gravity pulls it downward.

Try this

Try this experiment with gravity. You need two people, a small toy car, a sheet of stiff card, and a few books.

1 Lean the card against a stack of books to make a steep slope.

2 Fix it in place with sticky tape.

3 Hold the car at the top and let it go. Gravity will pull it down to the bottom.

Books

The card will bend slightly to make a curved track for the car.

Card

4 Now ask a friend to let the car go. Use your hand to stop the car near the top of the card.

5 Now try stopping the car near the bottom of the slope.

t's a fact

At the top, the car is going slowly. It hits your hand gently. At the bottom, it is going fast, so it hits your hand much harder. Ouch!

A skier picks up speed as they zoom downhill. Gravity pulls the skier downhill.

Slowing down

If you throw a ball, or push a toy car, it doesn't keep going forever. It slows down and stops.

You can see this if you push a coin across a smooth table top.

After you give the coin a push, it moves a little way. Then it slows down and stops.

The coin doesn't slow down by itself. A force is making it stop. This force is called **friction**. It happens as the coin rubs against the table.

Table top

coin

What happens if you try to push the coin on a different surface?

Try pushing the coin across a metal tray and a carpet.

Metal tray

carpet

You can climb up a rock face in rubber-soled shoes, because friction helps them to grip.

It's a fact

Smooth surfaces have less friction, so objects can slide on them more easily. Rough or rubbery surfaces have more friction, so objects grip them and slow down.

Useful friction

Friction is useful! The soles of your shoes grip the ground because of friction. Without friction, your feet would slide around. Friction helps your hands to hold things.

Try this

You need a plastic bottle, water, cooking oil, and an adult to help you.

1 Fill the bottle with water. It is heavy, but you can pick it up.

2 Now rub some oil on one hand. Try to pick up the bottle. What happens?

It's a fact

The oil makes it hard to grip the bottle, because oil has less friction.

When things rub against each other, friction makes them heat up. This is useful too.

Rubbing your hands together warms them up on a cold day.

Friction makes motorbike tires heat up and helps them grip the road surface.

Friction makes your hands warm when you rub them.

Try rubbing a cold coin on a smooth floor. Friction makes it get warmer.

Pressure

Pressure is a force that happens when one thing presses against something else. Air can be under pressure. The more it is squashed, the more it pushes back.

Ask an adult to blow up a balloon for you. Squeeze the balloon gently. It pushes back against your hand.

The air in the balloon pushes against your hand because it is squashed together under pressure.

Now blow up a balloon but don't tie it. Let it go. What happens?

The balloon zooms off around the room. The air inside it is pushing out of the open end. This pushes the balloon along.

WATER PRESSURE

Water has a pushing force, too. The deeper you go in water, the more it pushes in on you.

It's a fact

The air around us is under pressure, too. All the air above it is squashing it. Air pressure is pushing at us all the time. We don't feel it because we are used to it.

Machines

A **machine** is something that helps us to use forces to do useful things. Here's a simple machine you can make yourself.

Up

Try this
You need an eraser, a ruler, and paper.

1 Put the eraser on a table. Lay the ruler on top of it, so that one end sticks out further than the other.

2 Make a ball of crumpled-up paper and balance it on the long end of the ruler.

3 Now hit your hand down on the short end. What happens?

Long end

Pivot

Eraser

The short end moves down a short way, but it makes the long end zoom up a long way. The paper ball shoots into the air.

20

Paper ball

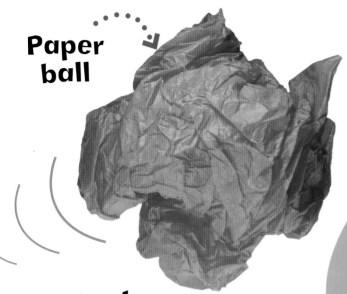

machines at home

We use hundreds of machines in our everyday lives. This screwdriver is being used as a lever to open a can of paint.

t's a fact

This kind of machine is called a **lever**. It can turn a short, strong movement into a long movement. Levers help to lift things.

The balancing point, where the eraser is, is called the **pivot**.

Ruler

Down

Short end

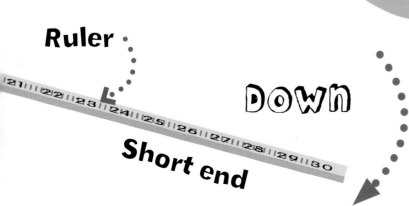

Glossary

Forces

Pushes and pulls that make objects start to move, slow down, change direction, or change shape.

Friction

A rubbing force that tries to stop surfaces from moving against each other. Friction slows moving objects and gives off heat.

Gravity

A pulling force that makes objects pull toward each other. The Earth's gravity pulls us toward it and stops us from falling off.

Lever

A simple machine that works by balancing a long stick on a point.

Machine

An object that helps us use forces to do useful jobs.

Pivot

The balancing point that a lever moves around.

Planet

A ball of rock and gases that circles around a star. We live on planet Earth.

Pressure

A pushing force that happens when something presses against something else.

Index

23

Notes for parents and teachers

• Point out ways in which forces make things happen in everyday life, and encourage your child to spot them. For example, you have to push a door to close it, and turn the handle to open it.

• Some things, such as cars, seem to move without being pushed or pulled. Discuss what might be making them move. The engine inside the car turns fuel into a rotating movement to push the wheels round.

• Ask children to think of ways in which we stop things moving or slow them down. How do parachutes, car brakes and train buffers work? See if you and your child can find out. Try making a parachute for a toy action figure.

• Gravity is working on us all the time. Discuss the ways it affects us, such as making grocery bags pull down on our arms, and pulling us down when we jump off a wall.

• Earth's gravity does not affect you when you are in space, and you can float freely. Ask children to discuss how they would hold objects down, keep control of food and drinks, stay in bed, or go to the toilet in zero gravity. Ask children to draw or paint a picture of themselves in zero gravity.

• Ask children to look out for objects with high friction that are designed to slow down movement or give a good grip. High-grip kitchen utensils, car tires, and bicycle brakes are good examples.

• Look out for different ways in which we use the pushing force of air or water, and point them out to children. Examples could be a garden hose, a bicycle tire, and a vacuum cleaner. Can you find out how they work?

• Look out for everyday examples of levers and discuss what we use them for. Seesaws and scissors are examples of machines that work using levers.